# THE SKY IS A NEST OF SWALLOWS

BELLEVILLE BOOKS PRESS
©2012 Belleville Books Press
FIRST EDITION

ISBN 978-0615607894 (Belleville Books Press)

Belleville Books Press is a nonprofit independent literary
publishing house. All proceeds from this publication will go
toward the continuing efforts of the Afghan Women's Writing
Project to enable Afghan women to find expression through
writing.

AWWP is dedicated to Zarmeena, a mother of seven who
was executed by the Taliban in the Kabul's Ghazi Stadium
on November 16, 1999, for allegedly killing her husband.

The writing included in this collection was previously published
on www.awwproject.com, a website that continuously publishes
new work by Afghan women writers involved in the Afghan
Women's Writing Project.

**www.awwproject.org**

# THE SKY IS A NEST OF SWALLOWS

## From Behind The Burqa:
## The Voices Of Afghan Women

A Collection of Poems and Essays by Afghan Women Writers
Written in the context of the Afghan Women's Writing Project

With an introduction by AWWP founder Masha Hamilton

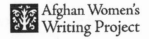 Afghan Women's
Writing Project

Compiled by Susannah E Pabot
On the occasion of the International Literary Festival
at Brown University
March 12-16, 2012: "Art as Sin"
The Middle East and Freedom of Expression

Cover art by Nazli Ceren Ozerdem
Design by Alexander Beer
Collection title adapted from an essay by Zainab

This publication was funded by
Brown University's Creative Arts Council (CAC).

All proceeds will benefit the ongoing efforts of the
Afghan Women's Writing Project
**www.awwproject.org**

[cac]

CREATIVE **ARTS** COUNCIL
BROWN

Journalist and novelist Masha Hamilton founded the Afghan Women's Writing Project in May 2009. She dedicated the project to the memory of Zarmeena, a mother of seven who was brutally put to death in Taliban-held Afghanistan before ever having the chance to tell her own story.

# Introduction

The Afghan Women's Writing Project started as a kitchen table idea in a Brooklyn brownstone, half a world away from the forbidding ranges of Hindu Kush, the arid poppy-fields of Kandahar, the Kabul roads where cars compete for space with burqa-clad women, donkeys and dust. The seed was planted, though, a decade earlier, when I first saw the grim image of an Afghan woman named Zarmeena being executed by the Taliban in the Kabul's Ghazi Stadium for allegedly killing her husband. Though a videotape of her Nov. 16, 1999, death was smuggled from the country, all that was known of her was that she had seven children and that her husband's family, mysteriously, had forgiven her.

This sobering blackout of information felt like a gauntlet thrown down for us all. Not only were women hidden beneath burqas, I realized, but their narratives were silenced. What little the outside world knew of what they endured through decades of war and years of oppressive Taliban rule seeped out only through the media or their men. Their own cries and laughter, laments and celebrations were as if swallowed by wind. That seemed a terrifying erasure, and a violation of human rights.

AWWP was founded in May 2009 to encourage and nurture Afghan women as they explore the power of their voices and reflect upon themselves, their histories and their possibilities. First with a single online workshop, and then with three workshops taught by rotating novelists, poets, memoirists and more, we began to prompt and urge and cheer on the Afghan writers.

We wanted their stories, but we knew we needed to be cautious. These women, in offering up their private thoughts and experiences for outsiders—Americans, no less—were embarked on an act of breathtaking courage within the traditions of their society. Some came from families that believed a woman who used a cellphone was a whore. Our growing volunteer team created a blog to feature their work, and we agreed: no full names, no sharing of emails, no specific locators.

It was clear from the start that the women wanted to write, but it would be wrong to call it an immediate opening of floodgates. They needed to believe that someone was at the other end, reading their work, and that we wanted to hear everything, the good along with the bad, the broad social concerns along with the breathtakingly intimate ones. Very soon, they grew comfortable, and lifted their burqas to reveal the feelings and experiences hidden beneath. The stories they told were haunting. Memories of being pursued by the Taliban while sneaking to secret schools. Of dragging an ill mother through the streets at night in a search for adequate health care. Of being robbed of a son at birth because a divorced father wanted a male heir. Of being caught in a firefight on the highway from Kabul to Kandahar.

They also wrote of fathers who encouraged them, moments of laughter, recipes they loved, the importance of prayer and of Allah in their lives. They wrote about the presence of foreign troops on their land. One wrote an open letter to President Obama, another to Secretary of State Hilary Clinton. They wrote about Afghan women in prison, life in refugee camps and, yes, they wrote about the burqa in all its complexity, a garment that causes Westerners to gape, but that often protects as it imprisons.

They did not want to be dismissed simply as caricatures of victims. In their own words, essay by essay, poem after poem, they have revealed the density and intensity of their lives. Many have said AWWP has been for them a gift, but it has been as big a gift for us. It has allowed us to see through the haze of war and of differences in culture and tradition to the amazing women of Afghanistan. We only hope that, were we presented with similar circumstances, we could meet them with as much grace, strength and optimism.

*Masha Hamilton*
*AWWP founder*
*February 2012*

# THE SKY IS A NEST OF SWALLOWS

History is changed by the small actions of ordinary people.
—Zahra A.

## Under Burqa
*By Seeta*

My face hidden, I smile, unseen.
It is I, Afghan woman, under burqa.
I try to be brave, show my presence.
See me, don't see me, but I am here.
I don't care how hot it is under burqa.
I am invisible.
I am part of my community.
I am here, Afghan woman under Taliban burqa.
I cannot use chader namaz— for I will be recognized,
My life threatened if they know what I do under burqa.
They will make me stop working, take my job, my life.
But I am an Afghan woman who wants to stay safe, continue my fight.
Yes, I am brave under burqa, enslaved in my generation of war.
Banned from education, my illiterate sisters cannot work.
Some hide, learn in home-based classes, still at risk.
Foreign women come to see us, under burqa, take our picture—
We are interesting, novel for them.
They don't understand our burqas are jail and safety made of fabric.
We are hidden beneath blue cloth, confined, yet secure.
I am Afghan woman, working under burqa. We are many
And if there is one, we are all Afghan women.
Insha'Allah, we will one day remove the burqa.
Yes, it is I, Afghan woman, under burqa—
Remember me.

## Read My Poems on the Reddish Stream of My Blood
*by Emaan*

I want to write, I want to write about
My dreams which never come true,
My power that has always been ignored,
My voice which is never heard by this deaf universe,
My rights which have never been counted,
My life decisions which are always made by others.
Oh my destiny, give me the answer, what am I for in this universe?
What does it mean to be an Afghan woman?
Hmm, I know you can't provide me with an elegant answer so
Just give me the pen, the *hidden pen*
So that I can write, that is all I am asking for!

I promise I will take revenge, but not like men
By gun and sword and aggression,
Instead I will write.
I will write even if I am warned not to touch a pen or paper,
I know one thing, that they can't see that hidden pen with their
Blind eyes, no matter how strong their vision.
My eyes will read my environment, my brain will save the details,
And I will write with the hidden pen on the chambers of my heart,
So that when I am caught and executed,
Perhaps in Ghazi stadium like other innocent Afghan women,
People can read my poems on the reddish stream made by my blood.

I will start writing with the hidden pen, and
I know this will lead to a day when girls of this land will be able
To write with chalk on the blackboards of the school
Or by markers on the whiteboards of universities,
And one day they will make their voice heard—
Then the hidden pen will be remembered forever!

## Always a Hand to Wipe Tears
*by Meena Z.*

I am from a land of bravery and beauty
A land surrounded by blue and silver mountains
A land where rivers searched and found their path in dignity

A land where poverty increases daily
Where death is cheaper than life
Where children die before they are born

I am from the blue sky of Kabul
The soft breeze of its air
The first dawn of its mornings that conveys a message of hope

I am from Afghan women who keep the name of Afghanistan alive
From parents who loved, cared, shared and worked hard for everything
From diligent and passionate siblings

From an American host family whose love and encouraging words
Always help me see the mirror of their wider vision
From an American grandfather whose support sustains me

I am from a social family for whom friendship is like a chain
Their love visible in their first and last breaths
I am from music, singing and dancing
From songs that carry me to other times
From loving nature and exploration and travel
From playing basketball with frozen hands on snowy days in
Ghazi Stadium

I am from soft breezes in the shiny sunshine of the spring
From the silver paths of the moon in summer,
From walking on golden maple leaves in autumn
From holding the fluffy snowflakes of the winter

I am from the second day of Eid, gathering with my relatives and friends
From the smell of my mom's qabuli palaw and kofta chalaw
From the soft essence of rose petals
From voices of hope and wisdom
From a land of kind hearts, where there is always a hand to wipe
My tears.

## A Garden Full of Flowers
By Sana S.

When I was a child my mom told my siblings and me a story about the war in Afghanistan, and how people were fighting with each other. "Why Mom, why, why?" I asked. "Because they do not know they are brothers and sisters," my mother said. "Killing and stealing are haram. They are forbidden," she told me. I felt so sad. I asked more questions and my mom told us everything about our country.

That night in bed I thought about why there was fighting. But I didn't get my answer. I fell asleep and dreamed that I was standing in a dark place full of smoke. After a while, I heard voices saying, "Help please. Help please."

I woke up. It was five o'clock in the morning and when I looked to my side, I saw my mom praying. She was saying, "Allah, please bring peace to our country and between our people." Tears came down her beautiful cheeks. When she finished, she looked around, but I pretended to sleep.

I hid under my blanket and told myself that after breakfast I would ask Allah to give me an answer. My mom used to say, "If you have a question, Allah will give you the answer."

I washed my face and hands, ate breakfast, and after that I closed my eyes and asked God: "Please tell me why fighting is going on in our country." After a second I heard somebody knocking on our door. My oldest brother had come from Afghanistan to tell us we should get ready to go to our beautiful country, "But in our country, there is war," I said. "I do not like Afghanistan."

My brother came next to me. I saw a smile on his face and he said, "No dear. Our country is so beautiful, but our people are blinded. They cannot see the beauty of our country and they do not know they are brothers and sisters." I had a smile on my face as I said, "I would love to go to my Afghanistan." My brother laughed. "No dear, not just your country, Afghanistan is for everyone." The day came, and my family and I were in the car on the way to our beloved country.

*I am going to Afghanistan*
*The place I have never seen in my whole life*
*I am going to see the mountains*
*Because our country is full of mountains*
*I will have lots of friends*
*But are they allowed to have friends?*
*I am going to see the beautiful places*
*But I am scared the Taliban will be there*

Tears came as I started to say, *Taliban, Taliban, Taliban.* My mom held me in her arms. "They will not harm us," she said. We went to live in Kabul. I met lots of people there from different tribes. I felt sad they would not help each other and they did not want to work with each other. *Why, why?* I thought to myself. We found a house for rent. In our yard we had a small garden with lots of flowers. I used to love that garden so much. It was a day in summer when I came home from school and I sat in our garden and with some bread wrapped in paper and started to eat like someone who had not done so for a year. As I looked at the beautiful flowers, my mom came and sat with me.

"How was your day?" she asked.

"It was great, Mom."

I looked around and saw a plant that did not have any flowers. "Mom, why does a plant look weird without any flowers on it?" I asked.

"Everything has its own beauty. When a plant has flowers on it, everybody wants it. People like to have them in their yards, because a life with flowers is beautiful and amazing. I have flowers in my life," she said. Then my mom told me that her children are her flowers.

*People do not care about a plant without flowers and they harm them so they won't grow again in their garden.*

After that conversation with my mom, I felt that Afghanistan was like a big plant and all the different tribes—Pashtun, Hazara, Tajik—are flowers.

*Right now we have a plant, but we do not have flowers,* I thought. The tribes are all separate from one another. If our people would come together like plants in a garden, then no one would be able to harm us and there could be peace inside our country. I am sure that was Allah's answer to my question. Our people are the beautiful flowers of our beloved land, Afghanistan.

Please pray for Afghanistan
The flowers that I am looking for
I think I will find soon.
The peace that I am waiting for
With tears and dreams will come soon.
I speak from the bottom of my heart
I love you, Afghanistan.
You will be beautiful again, like the past—forever.

## The Burqa
*by Meena Y.*

Navy blue, long and baggy
Top and bottom with different designs of flowers
Hanging outside the shop along with other white and green ones
Swinging in the cold wind of Kabul winter.
Swinging tiredly and wondering about the woman who would own it
Maybe the one who would wear it unwillingly
Cursing herself for being born a woman
Complaining about her inability to see or move freely.
Swinging right and left, the burqa remained wondering
Whose face would it hide?
Whose identity would it take?

## Have We Forgotten?
*By Meena Y*

My heart beats while listening to my friends talk of
Afghanistan and politics
My heart beats, but not from excitement
From fear.
It sees something my eyes are blind to see
It senses something my conscious refuses to sense
Islamism and fundamentalism are getting in fashion for our youth
Whether Afghan, Turk, Arab or Pakistani.
I want to reach out and shout
Have you forgotten the hungry Afghan orphans?
Have you forgotten the tearful eyes of Afghan mothers?
Have you forgotten the sight of a young mother burying her children,
The children she thought would bury her?
Can't your ears still hear the cries of Afghan children?
Can't you still feel the pain of Afghan women?
Can't you still see the amputees on the streets of Kabul?
Have you forgotten the nights that were followed only by nights?
Have you forgotten the songs of sorrow and the dances of death?
No, my people—for Allah's sake and for our own Muslim's sake
Let's not forget what extremism has done and can do to us.
Let's not forget the deaths, the rapes,
The hunger and the pain.

## Afghanistan, a Dream
by *Meena Y.*

I was standing in front of the window in the small, dark living room, folding my arms against my chest, looking out at the drops of rain falling like the tears of a mother for her dead child, like a gift from the hell, like a curse from the devil. The dark, gloomy sky had a rhythm of pain, a rhythm of loneliness. The land was like a woman in black, shouting from the unbearable pain. It was October 21, 2008. Taliban insurgents had pulled thirty Afghan men off a bus in southern Afghanistan and beheaded them after accusing them of being soldiers traveling in civilian clothes. The thirty were actually men going to west to Iran to find work. This was not only the end of thirty lives and their dreams, but the end for families and friends they had left behind waiting for them. I wanted to step back and leave the suffering, but the portrait inside my heart was no different from that of the view. I finally pulled myself away and closed my eyes, trying to see deep inside and imagine a dream picture of Afghanistan. I saw a land, warm from the sunshine, little girls and boys flying white kites in an open green field, dozens of women wearing green, blue and red scarves and sitting under the shadows of a pine tree, giggling while their noses shined from the reflection of sunshine, a group of men chuckling together. I saw a young man in white holding a little girl's hand with a pencil, teaching her how to write. I looked to the right side and there was a masjid (mosque) in the color of light emerald. I looked closer and found a woman wearing green head scarf reading to a younger girl from the pages of holy Quran.

I saw the same land in the winter with snow falling down from the sky like pearls, covering the land like a piece of white silk. It was pure like a gift from Heaven, like a blessing from Allah. I heard something, looked up, and it was the Snow Partridge sitting on the dry branches of olive tree covered with pure white snow, singing sola, sola and sola (peace, peace and peace.)

# And Nothing Less
by *Meena Y.*

The view of the bustling Pul Bagh Umumi district of Kabul was no different that windy day. The crowds of men and women looked as if they were walking on each other. Everyone seemed in a rush, as always. There were carts of green grapes, apples, peaches, and every other kind of fruit. Cart owners poured water on the fruit, making the colors flourish, giving life to the dusty, gloomy face of Kabul.

I looked at the faces passing by. There were happy, sad, and confused people, as well as faceless people. The faceless were the women in burqas, covered from head to toe. The thought of faceless people took me back to a picture in a German magazine I had seen years ago among my uncle's stuff when he was visiting from Europe.

The photo depicted a Muslim woman in a long black garment. Her face was hidden with thick, black cloth revealing only her eyes; her body was covered with a clear piece of see-through cloth. Not being able to read German, I looked at the picture for minutes, curious as to what it meant, a woman with a hidden face and a naked body. It seemed too much for my small brain to take in—or there was something I was too fearful to read.

Funny how life sometimes answers our questions not hours or months, but years later when we hardly remember the question. I have seen women in burqas all my life, but that day seeing them answered a question from the days of my innocence and childhood. It brought me to make one of the most painful confessions of my life.

Muslim women are forced to oppress ourselves according
to cultural and religious taboos so as not to be a sexual
distraction—and then to change into a prostitute the moment
the men want us to. It is ironic that in countries like Iran,
temporary marriage as short as three days is legal. Even in my
own country, they tried to pass laws that would require a woman
to have sex with her husband once every four days—otherwise,
the husband would have the legal right to rape her.

I find it ironic that a religion based on modesty and equality
for all has turned into an unjust and unfair system for its own
daughters. We Muslim women are punished at every stage of
our lives for the sole sin of being born female. We grow up
ashamed of our femininity, ashamed of our bodies and our
faces. We are sexually harassed every day by young men, old
men, men of all ages, the same men who have their own sisters,
wives, and daughters.

People are born free and equal and shall be granted the right to
liberty. I do not know if we can take our rights from our fathers,
husbands, brothers, and sons, but we can certainly insist, as our
American sisters did years ago: "Men, their rights and nothing
more; women, their rights and nothing less."

## My First Namaz
by *Meena Y.*


In the rainy season of Pakistan, the news
Of my grandmother's death made our lives rainier
This season showed me my father's tears for the first time
His red eyes hurt so much, I wanted to take the pain away
But didn't know how
After the long day of the funeral, he was sleeping on a mattress
I crossed my legs and sat close to him
My little hands touched his forehead; I put my head on his.
He woke up nervous as if he did not know where he was
He asked me how his love was doing. I said nothing,
But nodded my head
He went to pray for his mother's soul to rest in peace
I decided at age six, I was old enough to pray with him
I told him that God would listen to me more; I don't know
From where that idea came
He spread out two green prayer rugs
We both stood facing the qiblah
He took my small hands in his large ones
And put the right on the left, close to my chest
He asked me to repeat after him
As I bent, he helped me put my hands on my knees
And we stood up again
Now we both sat in Sajda, putting our foreheads on the rug
His head was still on the rug when I stole a glance at him
He looked back, reminding me that I was not supposed to do that
Looking the peace in his face, though, was probably worth the sin.

## Sky Is the Nest of Swallows
*by Zainab*


She was born in Iran and grew up with Iranian culture and
language. A flower needs soil to grow and for her, that soil was
Iranian. But her parents were Afghan immigrants—refugees—
and life was very hard. Privation, prejudice, strangeness: these
were daily problems.

She never thought it easy or even possible to separate a flower from
its soil—to say, "The soil is barbarian with you growing in it. It
doesn't know you! It doesn't like you! Go! Go to another place..."
So she could not believe Iran would persuade Afghan people
to return to their country. She felt herself an Iranian girl in
language, style, and culture. She could not face returning to a
country she knew nothing of except that people said she was
from there. She thought Iran was her home, her soil, but she
was wrong.

The family finally left everything in Iran and came to Kabul. So
many people had said goodbye to Afghanistan but they returned
to say hello, to say: "Hey, wake up! It is now time to recover, to
refresh, to stand up for us who came back for you."

During the first months, everything was new and life was good.
Her family pumped water from a well and looked at this as
useful exercise. Prices seemed cheaper because of the different
currency, and they felt more affluent. When there wasn't enough
fare for a bus or taxi they were happy to ride the rickshaw,
though it was dangerous and the rickshaw ride on Kabul's
bumpy Charqila Road was like a theme park ride.

One month, two months, three... a whole year passed, and

by then these things had grown boring. It seemed they had regressed ten years or more. It was no longer acceptable to waste energy and time extracting water from a well for washing clothes and dishes, instead of with piped water. The noise from the neighborhood kids became intolerable when the girl wanted to study. And in winter, she hated the snow, rain, and wind. The girl who used to love snowmen and drinking hot tea in the rain, who used to love the wind whiplashing her hair!

She had changed. The mud and slosh, the dust and pollution in the street made getting around, having electricity, and getting water much harder. Father's struggle to break wood for fuel and his trembling in the cold also changed her. Her tears when the wood was finished and there was no money to buy more—all of this changed her interests, ideas, even her appearance. She was now shy and her hands were black and wrinkled from the cold and dirty water of the well. She looked much older than her age. She endured her father's unemployment too. He had worked as a welder in Iran and he was covered with cuts and rashes that she sometimes had to soothe for him with pomades. So although they had less money in Afghanistan, she was glad her father's skin could heal. But he was ashamed about not working. He decided that an illegal return to Iran was the only solution.

She wanted the whole family to return to Iran but they didn't have visas so it was impossible. Only her dad went. They had never been separated more than a week. How could they tolerate this? God, how?

His hands were saints for her. She kissed them, these hands, which had taught her sacrifice and zeal. He lifted her head, looked in her eyes, and said: "Your father is strong, but do you know what my real power is? It is the hope of seeing my daughter in white doctors' cloth. You will make me proud. Remember this!"

\*\*\*

My father returned to Iran, that alien place. He returned because Afghanistan was also alien, both for me and for him. I will never forget how the Iranian people scoffed: Hey Afghan! Hey stranger! And I will never forget how the Afghan people, my people, also scoffed: Hey Iranian! Hey stranger! Neither country could provide fertile soil for our whole family.

It has been years since we returned to Afghanistan and I am still looking for a nationality. I'm still hoping for a piece of this earth where my family can sit down together. But my father has not returned. Sometimes I become sad and whisper: "God, I feel so poor not to have a home on any part of your earth!" At once a voice responds: "Don't be sad. You are more like a swallow than a flower. Swallows have no lifelong nest on earth. The sky is their nest. Do not worry. Reach for the sky!"

## We Will Rise
*by Pakiza*


We will rise like a bird in the blue sky of Afghanistan to bring peace
We will shine like a star in the dark sky of Afghanistan to bring brightness
We will rise like a sun to cover the darkness
We will stand like a stable mountain to reach our goals
We will plant like a gardener to raise our children
We will fall like a drop of rain to water our homeland
We will raise our hands to accomplish our dreams

## To My Loved One
*by Pakiza*

I wish ...
I could be the hands to touch you all the time.
I wish I could be your smiles to glow on your face
All the time.
I wish I could be your soul to exist with you all the time,  and I wish
I could be your memory to cling to your brain
All the time and I wish I could be your feelings to live in your heart
All the time.

I wish ...
I could be your body
To be with you
For the rest of your life.

# Dear Women of the World
by Pakiza

Over the years, I have met different people: all had something
to say and share, especially the women outside the Kabul
clouds. Some were amazing and some were so sad as to put
you in thoughts for days. Sometimes I couldn't find an image
for the women I met and I believe that Allah has given them
supernatural powers. Powers that don't only help them do
magic, but powers that made them Afghan women.

I am writing to people living outside our Afghan life. To tell you
what you never knew about, to change your assumptions about
Afghan women. We Afghan women don't always face the worst.
The times are gone when the women in Afghanistan have to sit
at home and wait for the male member to earn for the family.
Life was dreadful and a single beam of hope was more than
enough for us. Life changed and everything turned into hopes of
dreams and success.

The women got wings, letting them fly into the blue sky of
Afghanistan for the first time in their lifetimes. They got jobs,
they got parliament seats, they got school admissions, they
became media representatives, they became champions, they
became artists, they became role models, they became activists.
These are the Afghan women—women who faced hardness and
cruelty, but still didn't give up their struggle for freedom.

Life changes with a single stroke of struggle and we can reach
from the ground to the highest peak of the mountain. What we
are today—good or bad—we ourselves are responsible for it.
People in Afghanistan live a normal life going to jobs, attending

schools, picnics and parties, shopping and sightseeing. Bomb attacks, killings, these can never stop the Afghans from making their lives better.

The days are gone when we have to sit at home and blink at the bulb if there is no electricity. Now people will knock on the door of the electrical department asking why?

The days are gone when people are kicked out of their jobs. Now they will stand and ask why?

The days are gone when women are beaten up. Now they seek their rights, struggle for a better life, and ask the Afghan law to support them. This courage lies with some, but each drop of rain will one day turn into an ocean of dreams.

We are no longer weak. We are the mothers of the future and what mistakes our mothers made we will not repeat. We will not let anyone steal our dreams: we will snatch them back and tell them this isn't yours.

We will always empower ourselves and tell the male majority that we are no longer for sale.

We will choose what is for our good. We will not let others identify our needs and interests.

Women of the world, come and join Afghan women so they know they are not alone. We have the world behind us and we are living in our hopes. We have the international laws protecting us. We are the Afghan women.

With affection, love and hope,

Pakiza

## Saturn's Music
by Hila

I look at the night sky, wondering about you.
Are you from a far-off galaxy?

I live in this wreckage that the walls can't defend
This house can't hear the music of the New Year
The people of this house do not have the voice to sing
Anymore.
Where are you, dear alien?

My Earth is full of blood.  Are we searching
For you? Every day this beautiful weather
Comes and goes from across the mountains, crying and telling—

I haven't seen the green color of friendship—the color we lost—
For so long, and I am tired of this red. Between the war
And bloody streets, amid the pain of our land,
Where are the innocent? Where is the light?

At night I watch Saturn moving above my street
Incomplete and alone. You, too, dear alien,
Are alone.
If you can't come, send your smile
If you can't show your face, send your compassion.

My sky says, I am tired of crying.
This earth says, I am tired of crying.

Where is my real world?  Beautiful stranger,
Where are you? If someone sees you, dear alien spirit,
They will ask your name and wonder where you are from,
And can we touch your skin? We want to meet
You, but what do you want from us?

I have become just a body without a spirit—
Feet can't walk, hands can't hold, ears
Can't hear. The sun of my sky has disappeared—
Give the light back to us. Come morning, allow
Me to explain my wounds.

# Doorways
By Hila


The weather was rainy. My body shivered violently, but I couldn't move my hands. The whole place had an incredible stillness. Streets were hazy, and my eyes searched through the mist. I chose my steps carefully. I heard a voice and felt led to it, a whimper of a child looking at me. Her eyes were like bright stars, but behind the light was fear and grief. I peered deeply at her to uncover her secrets—when I moved closer, I found that her whole body was shaking and her feet were bare. She stood in the still, dark street.

She reminds me of my childhood. Of a time that I sat in a big enclosure, a closed yard. I didn't have the right to play with my friends. At every sound of a bomb that rang in my ears, I ran to my mother's arms. This dreadful sound became the song of my life that separated me from the world. Every time I tried to get out of the enclosure I couldn't. I tried to see outside the wall of our home, but I was scared. Even my dreams were not my own. Every night I dreamed that someone wanted to take my father from us, and he is the closest person to me. But among all these nightmares, a beautiful woman appeared, saying, "My daughter, this is life. " I would hide myself in the green trees and grass. My mother tried to calm me with sweet words, but during that time, among the bombs, I was crying and incapable of seeing everyone around.

I was a child, an Afghan girl who will always fight the difficulties of those years. Yes! I saw children in doorways, waiting for their mothers who were dying, who would never come home. I am a witness to a young boy who died, a mother's only child. I told myself, "I am a refugee child outside my country, I don't have the right to make choices, I must live poorly." I cried behind closed doors; my cold bed was full of teardrops. My mother sat next to me and said, "We will again have the right to hope for our country and for our lives. We will again wear new clothes in our country." But I can see that even in this green and beautiful world, girls still do not have many rights.

## Talk to Me
*By Shogofa*


I have come from a long way
Talk to me...
I am alone here
No mother, no father, no sister ...
I am new in your land.
I bring my country's story
I am tired from war
My ears are exhausted
I have lost my self
In crowds of people
Please talk to me?
I have come a very long way
Give me a smile?
I am tired of crying
I miss happy times
I miss my mother's hug
Talk to me ... for just a second?
I am new in your land
Hold my hand
Show me the way
I have lots to learn
I have lots to teach my people
Let's help each other
Bring peace and smiles on faces
I have come a long way
To start my new life
Please talk to me ...

## Let Me Grow Up
*By Shogofa*

Let me grow up
Let me talk
I have lots of words
Let me walk, so I may run and feel the earth
I am a prisoner
Let me see the world, share my pain with all
Let me tell how
I am a prisoner for long time
I have wishes
I have dreams as a human being
Let me reach the dreams
I lost in war
More than dreams,
I lost my identity
Where is it? How can I find it?
 I have been a prisoner for a long time
Let me see the world
Why must I stay in a cage?
The victim of so many rules.
Let me come out from my cage
See the garden of heaven
I am for living, not for beating
I am human before being an Afghan woman
I have been prisoner for a long time
Let me have my life.

## For Last and For Ever
By Shogofa

*For my mother, on the third anniversary of her death:*
Today was the day I saw you for the last time.
For the last time, you said goodbye and kissed me.
I heard your voice for the last time, the day you left me forever.
You taught me who I am— showed me my way.
I'm so far from you, yet every moment reminds me of being close.
Today was the day I saw you for the last time—
You kissed me, held and hugged me.
I hoped to see you again, to sleep, cradled in your arms,
But you left me for last and for ever.
I still wait to see your smile,
But today was the day you left me.
Nights pass, days pass too.
I miss you—can't say just how much.
Today was the day I saw your face
For last and for ever.
I kissed your hands today.
You said goodbye to me,
To life, took my smile with you—
For last and for ever.

# Eyes of My Burqa
*by Norwan*

World is a small word
From the eyes of my burqa
There is no geography
I can't see my right,
Nor can I turn to my left
Hot in the summer, cold in the winter.
Wearing a burqa,
I wear a tent
That hides my beauty
My mouth is blind
I have to eat my voice
My hands are locked in a cage
Sentenced to move or shake.
My legs too ashamed to walk
My long burqa sweeps the dust
I don't know who I am under the tent
My heavy burqa,
You can't see my pen
Nor my paper.
Under the burqa
I am an Afghan woman writer
Searching for a house of freedom.

## Take My Hands
*by Norwan*

Where can I talk?
Where can I tell my untold stories?
       Where
       Where
       Where
I speak from under my burqa
I am not allowed to speak aloud
I am an Afghan woman
I breathe poisons.
I am not allowed to breathe the fresh air you breathe
I look outside the windows of my burqa
It seems as if there is
No hope
No light
I see nothing but hopeless dreams
I see nothing but
       Darkness
       Darkness
       Darkness
It seems as if the doors of victory are closed
       Locked
       Locked
       Locked

There is no door in the jungle of wild thoughts.
I want a light to see my way
I want nothing else but
        to live the way I want to live
        to live the way I deserve.
I want to release myself
From the prison of a voiceless land.
From the tribe of silent
        Dead
        Burned, women
Help me.
Take my hands.
It is not written in my destiny
To burn myself.
Can you hear me?
I am a voice of my dead silent generation
I speak from under my burqa
I am not allowed to speak aloud
        Where can I talk?
        Where can I tell my untold stories?
Where can I buy a light?

# The Voice of Sahar Gul
*by Norwan*

Every time I write, I decide that this time I am going to write something nice, interesting, funny, and happy. I think, this time, I am going to paint the happiest moments of an Afghan woman's life. I wish there was a happy scene for me to tell. I wish there were scenes of brightness and laughter inside the lives of Afghan females. I search and research—but I find so much sorrow. In writing this story I must eat my tears and anger. I try not to cry, so I can write it for you—for you, dear readers. You would never think human beings could be this wild, that human beings can do such violence to one another. Recently, a fifteen-year-old girl was released from imprisonment after five months. Sahar Gul was sold by her family and forced to marry an Afghan army soldier. Sahar lived in Baghlan province in the north of Afghanistan and she was kept in the basement of her house. Her in-laws tried to force her into prostitution. She did not accept this, and struggled to ignore what they forced her to do. They then beat her wildly and ripped her fingernails out, tortured her with hot irons, and broke her fingers. All her body parts were bruised and bloodied with black scabs.

Sahar was released after five months in the basement of her house. Her relatives called the authorities and told them about her, and then helped to get her to Kabul. She is in the hospital now and her story went to the media. Looking at her pictures, I can't stop my hate for wild, ignorant families and the men who inflict such violence on women. Sahar Gul is one of thousands of women who share the same destiny. She was lucky she was released. Although she remained silent, tolerating pain and torture, she became a voice for other women. Girls and women tolerate violence and accept it as their God-given destiny because they are women. They remain silent and voiceless because if they tell their stories nobody will accept them at home again. With such struggles these women don't actually live; they miss all of life's beautiful moments. There is no doubt that Afghanistan is the worst place for women. Writing about such stories I doubt that we are Muslims. In Afghanistan most of the marriages are arranged and forced. Families decide, and girls are like sculptures, bodies without soul. This is true. They can't decide their future and can't stand up to the mad traditions and wild decisions of their families. Of course forced marriages are never successful and then the families say to the girl that it is your destiny and God gave you this kind of life. They say you must accept it and face it while you are alive and God will reward you in the other world.

Sahar Gul's mother-in-law was arrested by the police because she ignored the violence against Sahar. I don't know where Sahar will go after she is treated. I hope she will be safe, but it is very hard for women once the story goes to media. Then nobody will accept her back at home.

Looking at the lives of women in my country makes me cry every night and creates questions in my mind. I ask God: "Are you the enemy of Afghan women? Is it you that gives us life and faith? Why is life always so unlucky and full of torture?"

## Chocolate-Flavored Days
*By Norwan*

My sweet sweet
Chocolate-flavored days
Of playing everywhere
Running like horses, jumping like deer
Drawing the sun in the mud
Counting the stars at night
My childhood, my cute days
Come again, hug me again
Just like the time mum did
Childhood!
I love to see your face
Forget the burdens of the world
Play with the kids
Think about if mum is awake
If she will comb my hair with her fingers
I laugh and play by myself
Then I cry: Mummy!
Where is my cradle?
I am tired of this world.

## Survival
by Mina M.

Time gets old.
I hear your voice behind the wall.
When the curtain is drawn,
You surrender to a muddied world.
Can you see who you are,
In prison, wishing for freedom?
Pain cannot relieve pain.
Can you hear my voice?
Who can rescue you?
Can you stand?
Veils are everywhere.
Up in the hills, there is a way.
The truth of the tulip
Will one day be revealed.
Look at the moon—
Its light illuminates your face.
Listen to the wind—
Your voice is there.
Stand on the path, and look behind.
Who knows the end?
You must survive.

# I Prefer to Be Called a Woman
*by Seeta*

On a day when it was very cold and windy, the wind brought the news of a child who was not yet in the world. Soon it would be time for the child to be born, entering into a world of expectations. Until then, maybe this child did not know where it was going, or why, or what people would expect from the child. A family also waited to hear from the doctor. And there was a pregnant mother waiting for her child. She had not thought about the pains she was suffering, because she was worrying. She had lost two daughters already, yet she had to have a child because her in-laws were violent. That is why her daughters had died. After one hour in hospital, the nurse came and told the mother in-law, "Congratulations! You have a grand-daughter." The mother-in-law said, "Thanks to Allah for giving us this gift although it is not a son. It is okay it is a daughter."
This child was me, Seeta.
Because I was a girl, the mean words and violence began towards me at that time. When my uncle who was only 11 went to tell my aunts about my birth, they responded: "Thanks for the news, but this is not a son." Or they said, "My poor brother, after years he got a daughter. Oohhh, daughter, daughter...."
This was not my sin or my mother's sin. This was the sex that Allah gave to me. It is not changeable by a mother.
As years passed and I grew up, my father loved me a lot; my mother too. But the other people—my uncles and aunts and even the neighbors—they used to tell my mom she is very unlucky to not have a son.

My mother was educated and she responded, "I am young and maybe Allah will give me a son." This became a dream. Her second and third children were born, but they were daughters. We three sisters always were disappointed that none of us was a son, but my father said, "I raise my daughters the same as boys, even better." People did not stop their bad words against us. Nobody thought about how if we believe in Allah, then we should accept Allah's wishes.

As I grew up I was very sad. I even hated myself for being a girl and, in the future, a woman. When I reached seven years old, I told my father, "Dad, you should not worry that you do not have a son. I will work for you the same as a son and then people will say to you, 'Ohhh what a brave daughter you have.' " My father smiled and said, "My dear, you are right. You are also human and have power, but you never can change to a son and it is very difficult for you to do the work that a son can do." I told him, "Yes, Father, you are right. Possibly I cannot do the same work that a son can do, but I will be a help for you in the future." My father did not say anything and left me with a world of my childhood wishes. He sent me to school. I was in love with my school. In the first grade I became the third student with 95 percent marks. My father was very proud. My uncle's sons were uneducated. When the Taliban took power in Afghanistan I had to stay at home like other girls.

We left for the city of Nimroz where my father had opened a small shop. The shop was far from our house and every day I took my father's lunch to him. After lunch he used to leave the shop so he could go to the mosque for his prayers. I was the younger shopkeeper. The other shopkeepers were surprised at how I managed the shop and sold things to the customers.

After Nimroz we left for Iran. During that time I helped my father when he was traveling to do his business. Because he was an Afghan he was not allowed to work, but I dressed like an Iranian and I was a child, so police were kind and did not say anything while my father did his work. At that time we three sisters were studying in Iran. At home we worked by cleaning pistachios to help our father.

For years and years I was a support to my father: shopping, working, and studying. I have done a lot to show my father I can do the work that a son can do.

My father was happy in front of me and my sisters. But outside the family he was not happy. His mother and brothers wanted him to marry again. When we heard this—me and my sisters and my mother—we sat at home in a dark room. We could only cry and cry that Father has to have a son.

Who can change Allah's decision?

The girl's family changed their mind and told my father, "You have three good, educated daughters. You can live with them." My father changed his decision to marry again after that.

After the fall of the Taliban regime we came back to Afghanistan. We had no house and my father did not have a good salary so I decided to find a job. A project was opening in my province where they needed teachers to teach adult students. I was 15 and in ninth grade, but I went for the interview. I succeeded because I had studied in Iran. In the morning I went to school and in the afternoon I taught my class. My students were older than I, but I enjoyed teaching them, and with my salary we could have enough food.

When I graduated I did not pay attention to my higher education because of economic problems. I started work. I helped my father to buy a small house—it was ours—we could live there without problems. Then we got medicine for my mother, and then we bought a car. Not a very expensive car, but it can take us somewhere. After years, my uncles and my aunts said, "Your daughters are better than my sons. We have sons, but we do not have a good life like yours."

After years and lots of violence against us, now they say that there is no difference between boys and girls.

But it is very late. My mom suffered problems from all the violence; we never felt happiness because of our gender. I now have a brother too. He was born after 17 years in Afghanistan and he is three years old and so lovely. When I go to ceremonies my cousins no longer tell their friends that we do not have a brother. Today I am happy that I was born a daughter, not a son. Some of my friends say to me, "Seeta, you are a man, not a woman." But I say, "I prefer to be called a woman."

## The Scent of Sweet Honey
by *Aisha*

Her name is Nelofar, and she is my cousin and my best friend. She had a love marriage, rare in Afghanistan. One day I asked her how much she loved her husband. Nelofar said, "I love him so much that I can feel him near me right now."

"What do you mean?" I asked, because her husband was nowhere near her; in fact he was not in the country.

She looked at me, smiling, and answered with three words: "By his smell." I started laughing out loud. Then she explained and I listened as if she were telling me a fairytale.

"Every time I pass the flower shop on my way to work, the smell of the flowers reminds me of him and I stand there feeling how close he is to me right now, how sweet he is and how wonderful he is."

She looked at me, knowing I was wondering if she meant all the flowers, but she immediately added: "The smell of jasmine and the smell of red roses mixed together somehow it gives you the smell of... um... sweet honey. And you can never have enough of that smell."

Nelofar had those two flowers on her dining table where we were sitting; I tried to smell the sweet honey, but the only thing I smelled was jasmine. "Every time I pass that flower shop, I stand there for almost two minutes, smelling it and feeling him close to me," she went on. "The smell of jasmine reminds me of the day we first met. I was sitting in a park and there were a lot of jasmine bushes. He sat next to me near the bushes. He began to smell like jasmine, and he had the smell on him the next morning too. The next few weeks when we met, he brought me red roses with jasmine flowers around the red roses—he knew I love jasmine a lot—and the funny thing is that these two flowers combined to make the smell of sweet honey. When we got married and I got closer to him, he actually had the scent of sweet honey. Now that he is away, every time I pass the flower shop I stand there and smell the scent and it reminds me of how we met, every time we spent together, every second we cherished, every word he said, his every touch, his every kiss."

I looked at her and I saw how she was lost in her story and I let her enjoy her daydream. Then I called her name, but she didn't answer me; she was gone in thought, looking at something in midair. I clapped my hands in front of her face so hard, Nelofar jerked out of her chair, and we laughed. The rest of the day went by just like a blink of an eye. Suddenly Nelofar reached for her heart and started breathing fast. I was frightened and didn't know what to do. I reached for her hand and she looked up at me and said, "He's ... he's here."

"How do you know?" I asked, raising an eyebrow. "I ...I ... I can feel him. He is here ...." Nelofar started breathing faster now, and I didn't know what to do. Then she got on her feet and ran to open her apartment door and there he was standing in his black suit. He was not so tall, his black hair was combed and he looked clean. I decided to give them some privacy.

# Destiny Awaits: A Lyric Essay
*by Nasima*

*1983 Afghanistan: Farah Province Balabluk District: Shewan village*
Tank fire overwhelms the Soviet plane.

There are children, children young and old.
They are killed. So many, so many babies gone.
Breast milk is meant to feed and keep the children safe.

There are mothers, mothers young and old.
They cry. So hard, such sound.
The blood. The will of God and the sky.

The mother calls for her baby. She stares, her eyes watching everything.

Her baby remains opaque.

Dark night is everywhere, silent, secret.
Two women and two men and three children, leave Shewan for Iran.
They travel, lost in the dark night, silent, secret.
Forty-five nights.

*Afghanistan: Farah Province: Deheshk village*
The eyes and minds of a bright future stare across the border.
No one knows his destiny.
The driver uses a white light. Voices. Soviet tanks. Helicopters.
Border Crossing:
Voices, like monsters in the desert. Clanging chains.

Faces red with anger.
Questions, day and night. Questions for the runaways.
Answers—are they lies or truths.

Oh Iran! We are your refugees.

*Iran: Mashhad Province: Shamshabad village*
The refugee camp is dry. There is little water.
Hungry, thirsty, homeless, poor.

The man hopes to live again.
Red sleeves up, he builds a house of mud and straw for his family.

*1985 Shamshabad village*
A child born.
Away from war, she is unfamiliar with misery.
Destiny awaits, once again.

# Childhood Memory: Zainab's Death
*by Marzia*

When I was ten years old, I was a student in a tailoring shop. In my teacher's neighborhood there lived a family with one son and one daughter. Their son was 7 and their daughter was 14. In our culture, girls are not allowed to have boyfriends or relations before they get married. But this family's daughter had a boyfriend without telling anyone about it. The girl's name was Zainab; she made a friendship with the boy next door who was 16. One summer afternoon these two went to the trail and slept together. After that the girl got pregnant and everyone knew about that. Her parents became very sad and ashamed for their daughter's mistake. Unfortunately, most of the time in our culture, when something like this happens, all the suffering and sorrows are for the girl, not for the boy.

Zainab's mother went to the boy's family and asked her mother to let his son marry her daughter. The boy's mother did not accept and said that her son was not going to marry her ugly and bad daughter. She told Zainab's mother: "If you are feeling sorry for your daughter, why didn't you teach her not to hang out or sleep with the boys?" The girl's mother became very sad and angry. At that time Zainab was five months pregnant. The mother came home, took a big stone and put it on her daughter's belly and killed her.

After killing their daughter, the family moved from that area. Sometimes people saw the boy at the girl's grave crying. He was a handsome boy with blue eyes, and the girl was cute with brown skin.

I heard Zainab's mother became very sorry for killing her daughter, but it was too late. She had not controlled her anger. Now the boy has a wife and children, but the poor girl, she lost her dreams and life. It was one of my childhood's bad memories. It makes me very sad. Every day many such cases happen in Afghanistan. People remember these for a while, but very soon they forget everything.

## A Father's Choice
*by Nadia*

Once upon a time there was a large family with ten members.
They were so poor they couldn't live normally. Sometimes they
didn't have any food to eat. In this family, only the father could
work because the children were small, and couldn't work. The
father didn't know what he should do. He couldn't buy food and
clothes for their children.

One day he met a man who had a drugstore. He told him about
his life. The man gave him a suggestion.

At first the father got sad and refused to consider it. But when
he came home the poor man saw his children who were waiting
for their father to bring them some food. But he had come home
with empty hands. The children became desperate.

The man sat in the corner of the room and thought about his
friend's speech. "You have eight children and can sell the kidney
of one of them and get a lot of money."

The man could not sleep. The next morning when his friend
opened his drugstore, the man went to him and told him his
decision. The next day his friend took one of his children and
they went to the doctor.

The boy was so afraid when they went to the doctor's room.
After an hour the doctor came out and said, "We could take the
kidney but couldn't help the boy. Unfortunately, he died."

## How Can I Hide My Sorrow?
*by Farahnaz*

I am an Afghan girl,
Tears in my eyes, pen in hand,
Writing from my heart.

That heart, full of sorrow,
Pain, grief, sores.
How can I hide my sorrow?

No one understands me
Or feels my sadness.
No one smooths ointment on my wounds.

How can I hide the sorrow
That fills me,
When my heart is
Exploding
      Exploding
            Exploding

## Fatima, Victim of Caprice
*By B.Fatima A.*

One day while at the house of the woman who bakes dough into bread, I ran into Fatima. I hadn't seen her in many years, but she had kept in contact with my mother. The line for turning dough into nan was long, so amid the warm, comforting scent of baking bread, we began to talk in a corner of the room away from the ears of others. Fatima told me her story, which I repeat below:
"I lost my mother when I was 18 and was the only girl in my family, living with my father and seven brothers. I worked as a tailor earning enough money to satisfy any personal needs. My father, a civil servant, was kind and did not press me into accepting any of the many marriage proposals that came my way. I did not tell my father, but I had my own idea of the type of man I wanted to marry—my very own dream person. I was determined I would hold out marrying until I met the person who was exactly like the one I had created in my mind.
"My life was pleasant and relatively ordinary until one quiet evening; I was working on a special sewing job when there was a knock at the front door. Looking at the clock, I realized this was about the time that my second brother Farhad should be home from work. I was proud of Farhad because he had just completed his college education. I had no idea how the knock on the door would change my life. I was surprised to see Farhad standing at the door with a girl who was holding a suitcase. I couldn't imagine why Farhad had knocked, but I did not want to be impolite so I invited the girl in while looking quizzically at Farhad.
"By the look on his face, I started to have an inkling as to what

was about to happen but I did not want to believe it. Farhad asked me to go tell our father that he needed to speak with him, and to make sure all of our brothers came into the room. I guess my father had seen them from window, because he burst into the room in his bare feet. Farhad stepped in front of the girl and announced 'She escaped from her father's house to be my wife. She is now my wife.'

"That Farhad showed no shame to my father did not surprise me, knowing Farhad. But I could tell by the looks on my brothers' faces that no one could believe it. Everyone in the family was frozen in their spots, not knowing what to say or do. While we were all staring in mute silence, Farhad went to his room with his new 'wife.' No one stopped him. We didn't know what to do and there really wasn't anything we could do.

"The first week in the house was strange and strained. Saleha, Farhad's wife, did not speak to anyone but Farhad. Farhad did not seem to notice the unease that had fallen over the house. One day I overheard Saleha whispering to Farhad that she was afraid that her brother or father might find her. Farhad seemed confident that nothing would come of Saleha's fears.

"One night about two and a half weeks later, the front door of the house burst open and Saleha's father and her brothers entered like wild animals jumping out of a cage. My father welcomed them into the house and offered them tea. As I brought the tea, my father tried to calm them down. Saleha's brothers were yelling so loudly I was sure that the neighbors were aware of what was taking place in our house. I had thought Saleha's family might be a little respectful because Saleha had gone willingly with Farhad. It was not as if she was kidnapped or coerced.

"After bringing the tea, I listened at the door, becoming angry at the way they were talking to my father with a harsh accent. I wanted to go into the room and remind them that they were talking to a human being, he was my father, it was his house and they were being disrespectful. I was getting madder by the minute as I listened to the cruel strong voice of Saleha's father. Then I heard Saleha's father say: 'Since your son has done this with my daughter, either your daughter should marry my son....' I became absolutely still; I dried up inside. I thought I am like a wood that they use to heat the room, no matter what. They want me to marry their son, to bring peace. In the haze of my thoughts I heard Saleha's father continue, 'So it will be equal and I will be sure that you will not be cruel to my daughter, plus if you do anything to her I will do the same to your daughter when she becomes my son's wife. The other option is that I will kill every single person in this house plus anyone who tries to defend you.'

"I fainted when I heard the last part of Saleha's father's threat. I did not know how my father or brothers responded. When they had gone, my father found me on the ground. He took me to the closest clinic. I came to after two hours. When I realized where I was, I began thinking about what had happened. I wanted it to be a dream but I knew it wasn't. I didn't know what the final decision was, but I knew I never wanted to lose my father or anyone from our house. I told myself I had to accept what had happened and sacrifice my life to bring peace. I didn't expect this to happen to me in any point of my life. But I had to accept that you never know where your destiny takes you.

"When my father came into the room I could see the sorrow in his eyes. As he entered the room he paused. I said: 'Salaam, padaar jan'; he answered very weakly: 'Walekom bassalam dokhtarm.' I tried to pretend that nothing had happened. So I said 'Chetor hasty padaar jan?' (Translation: 'How are you dear father?') He nodded his head as a sign of fine. I could read my father's face; I knew him too well. He didn't pick his head up during the whole time that I was talking to him. He told me the result of the conversation with Saleha's father. He said he didn't have any other choice than to accept the deal. 'He would've killed everyone, because he is very powerful,' my father said as his eyes filled with tears.

"I was engaged within a week. Fortunately, my engagement lasted for two years. During those years, I tried to spend a lot of time with my father. When we were alone in the house, he would talk with me about my future with my in-laws. I would begin to cry and my father would cry with me. Sometimes we would talk and cry for hours and not realize it. My father tried to give me confidence for the day when I would leave his house. He assured me that I would not be treated badly because their daughter would be in our house. But I could tell by my father's eyes that he did not believe what he was saying. We both knew that bad days were waiting for me. Sometimes my father would come home and find me crying. He would leave again to avoid my crying, which would make him cry. During those two years I watched my father grow old with sorrow. He became as old in two years as he would've been in ten years. He suffered a heart attack from the sorrow that surrounded us.

"My engagement time ended and I had to marry. During the marriage ceremony I tried to look happy for my father. I had a strange feeling that if people live for better, I was about to begin living for worse.

"My first week of marriage did not begin well. It seemed as if my new family had made a list of my weak points. They pointed these out and teased me about my brothers and their lack of income. I was determined to be tolerant and accept what was doled out. I told myself that I believed that 'When a girl marries and goes out of her father's house, she should come back with a shroud,' or only after she is widowed. I wanted to be strong for my family.

"If I thought the first week was not going well, it was heaven compared to what waited for me during the second week. My husband's family told my husband lies about me. My husband never asked for my side of the story. When he came home, he would enter the room and begin yelling at me. Then he would hit me with his belt. He hit me so much that I was not able to stand for three days, and I couldn't talk for one full day. Beating me with the belt was to become part of our marriage. My beatings averaged about once a week. Afterwards I would be unable to stand for at least a day, sometimes for two.

"I never told my father about the beatings. I always told him that everything was fine and then would cry for hours afterward. I kept everything inside, way down deep inside. I would dream of going into the desert and shouting very loud letting it all out. But I didn't, I couldn't, I had no one to share my sorrows with. I had no way to get the grief and turmoil out of my mind.

"My father passed away after five months of my marriage. I felt as if I lost everything with him. I had no one in the world except for Allah. I started talking to him more and more. I would often ask him about my father.

"One day a few months after my father's passing, my husband entered the room. He asked me why I didn't listen to his mother? I told him that I hadn't seen his mother during the whole day, but he didn't listen to me. He hit me so hard with a thick piece of wood that blood was pouring out of my legs.

"The next night my husband and his family went to a wedding. Reshad, one of my husband's brothers, was left to guard me. I told Reshad I needed to do some grocery shopping. He didn't want to take me, so I suggested that he go. I promised to stay home as I had a lot of housework to do. At first Reshad was hesitant, but I was so insistent and could point out all the chores that needed to be done, so Reshad finally gave in and left, saying he would return in a few hours with the groceries.

"When Reshad had been gone for a safe amount of time, I left the house. The moment I stepped out of the house, I felt as if I had become free from jail. I headed for my father's house. I knew that my husband's family would come to take me back to their home. I did not care. At that moment, I was free. As I made my way to my father's house, I looked up at the sky, breathing deep breaths of air, and spoke with Allah.

"About 10:30 the next morning, there was a knock on the door. My heart pounded but I did not let it show. I sent my brother to open the door. As I expected, it was them, wanting to take me back to their house. I stood tall and calmed my pounding heart. I said: 'I will never ever return to your house.' So they took Saleha to their house, whether Farhad wanted it or not.

"After they left I asked myself: 'What should I do now?' then decided I would live in my father's room. In this room I can remember my father crying when I was sad, laughing when I was happy, telling me that I was his angel, and a princess. I asked Allah to take me to where my father was, but he would not.

"It has been twelve years since I returned to my father's house. My brother Farhad has nine children now, but he doesn't have a happy life. He doesn't like his wife and he doesn't trust her. He likes another girl and wants to marry her. I work in their house—my father's house—like a servant. I've had many marriage proposals since I came back from my husband's house, but I don't have any good memories from my first marriage. I will never marry again.

"I see my father in my dreams very often and I talk a lot with him; now he knows everything that happened to me in those six months. He says that he didn't believe me when I told him that I was happy there. He says that he knew everything even when he was alive. He always says that he is 'proud' of me, and those are the words I am living with."

Fatima had come to the end of her story. Her beautiful face belied the last twelve years as she handed the woman her dough for baking.

## My Mother Speaks About Her Pregnancy
*by Fattemah AH.*

I feel something strange inside me
The days are more beautiful
Whenever I touch my belly
I feel you inside me, my daughter – moving
Month by month my belly becomes bigger
It's so strange
This is the first time I've had this kind of feeling
I feel I am a woman
With you inside me
I feel I am more grown up now
With you, I know my world
Will not be the same as before
You are a big change in my life
Now, I feel I smell different too
I smell like a blossomed flower
With you inside me.

## Grandma's Kitchen
*by Yagana*

Crowded as a fish market
With walls as white as a glass of milk
It is a place of love
Where everyone helps each other
Old dishes from her childhood
But more modern than before
It is a place of kindness
Where things are kept very clean
And young girls hold their secret chit chats
And give advice to each other
That is my Grandma's kitchen.

### The Garden of My Homeland (Clothed in Blood and Fear)
*by Sabira*

I am a daughter who has witnessed sixteen springs and the nests
Of beautiful swallows in those winters.
In the spring, all beauty and blessings rain onto the earth.
Like in my father and mother's house where it rained the blessing of God.

I am a daughter who was born into a big family
Of unschooled parents who still gave special importance to education.
They provoked the flame of knowledge in their babies.

I am a daughter who was born into the heart of Asia at a moment when
Everywhere was clothed in blood and danger and fear.
My mother feared for me all the time.
Every family mourned for their dear children.
Guns and missiles were the voices mothers heard
Instead of their children's babbling.

My family emigrated as refugees to neighboring lands.
When we returned to our homeland, its beauty was gone.
It had changed to a desolate place.
Bloodshed and the sound of crying was everywhere.
Friendship between people had been forgotten.

I was able again to enter into the garden of education
And pick some flowers.
I benefited from that garden.
My family praised me as I grew day by day.

I came to understand my homeland was sick and desolate.
I knew I must help transform it.

My teacher said: "You are the future.
You are the gardeners of your homeland."
Remembering that, I made myself a garden.
I made myself a gardener and I've learned to irrigate.

In my mind, I see a beautiful homeland, one far from war.
When I walk the streets of my homeland;
I remember nightingales at dawn.
I sing for the improvement of my homeland.
I give my childhood and youth to develop my homeland,
The place I call my own.

# A Pretty Toy in My Family's Hands
*by Anonymous*

I was sixteen years old, attending school and thinking about my future goals to be either a doctor or a journalist. I knew nothing of life, and I had no thought of marrying. One day my uncle, who is a doctor, came to our house and said, "You should not study, because you are a girl. You should get married." I thought it was a joke because my uncle is a doctor and knew the value of education. I come from an educated family; almost all my relatives were educated. I was polite and said nothing. I got him tea, and then went to do my homework.

The next day, several relatives arrived at our house. I was not aware at first of what was going on, but then I understand they were at my home to buy me. I was such a pretty toy, a pretty toy to play with. The family that was proposing the marriage was discussing my cost with my father. At that time, I did not know I had any right to say I was not for sale.

Finally, they sold me for 6,000 US dollars. This is when my life problems started. My fiancé was uneducated and he forbade me to go to school. After one year, when I was seventeen, my husband divorced me, but I was already pregnant.

My baby arrived prematurely. The night he was born, I nearly died. It was a very bad night. All the doctors were working to save me and my child. My body was in a lot of pain, and I had no information about becoming a mother. When the midwife handed me my newborn, I remember she said, "You are still a child. Why do you want to give birth to another child?"

After the birth, my ex-husband took my son and left me with

nothing. Here again, I did not have information. What should I do? I didn't know. There was nobody to tell me, "It's your right to take care of your own child." Again, my family played with me. After one year, I began to work and started my new life. I understood the things that were done to me were completely wrong. But I didn't fully feel my anger. I worked in my province for four years. Then I decided to continue my education, and I asked my office to transfer me to another province, because in my province it was not possible for me to study.

I moved and began school. And one day, our teacher was giving a lecture about psychology. He was talking about marriage and he said that in Afghanistan, some parents do not think about the health of their daughters; they try to get them started on married life early, so girls who are sixteen years old get pregnant, and in this way they become ill or even lose their lives, and the life of the children is also difficult, often filled with illness, when they are born to a mother so young.

In my class, nobody knows about my past. I have told them nothing because it is Afghanistan and if they knew what happened, they would not respect me. If they knew, I would have to suffer as I did in my home province, where they called me "the divorced woman." But during this lesson, I went back into my past and thought about what had happened to me when I was a child and knew nothing.

When I think about it now, I get too angry. At one point, I felt hatred toward my family because they had treated my life like a pretty toy. I was without information, but the elders had to know I was not ready to get married. They played with me and my life, and I had to respect their decisions even when those decisions were against my own future.

I wanted to fight their choices for me, but I was without knowledge, and so the problems from my past life remain with me until today. But now, I have a dream to start a program for women to let them know about these problems. I want to save other women. I hope those who read this story would help me continue on this job to teach young girls in the far-away districts of Afghanistan about their rights. I want all women to come with me and support me in this goal.

## Baad
by *Salma*

Fatima was playing with her friend and cousin in her grandfather's lovely flower-covered garden. As she caught sight of many of the older villagers entering the house, she thought that her father must be throwing a party. She had no idea that her family was busy making the most important decision of her young life.

At just 14 years old, Fatima was a very pretty and innocent girl with beautiful eyes. What Fatima did not know was that her brother had ruined her life. He had killed a neighbor's son, and Fatima would pay the price. The villagers had decided Fatima would have to marry Jan Mohammed, a man who was thirty years older. She was to pay the price of baad, an Afghan tribal tradition that involves giving a victim's family a member— usually a girl—of the offending family.

When Fatima's family told her the news, she cried a lot. She knew she was the victim of her brother's crime and she did not have a choice. If she refused to marry Jan Mohammed, then her brother or another family member would be killed. This would continue until all were killed. Fatima hoped she would get lucky. Sometimes in the case of baad, in-laws can be nice. Most of the time, though, new brides were treated as servants.

On her wedding day, despite the fact that Fatima was a beautiful bride, she was sad and worried about her future. But to her surprise, Fatima found Jan Muhammad's family was very nice to her. Jan Muhammad was smitten by Fatima's beauty and fell in love with her. Soon Fatima returned Jan Muhammad's feelings and fell in love with him too. After a year of marriage, a baby boy was born. Fatima's new family was very happy that they had their first grandson. They named him Ahmad. Ahmad was as handsome as Fatima was beautiful.

But Fatima's happiness with her new baby and family was to be interrupted. One night in a bombing, Fatima lost her family—her brother, sister, father and mother all died. What saved her from complete sadness was Ahmad, watching him grow and learn new things day by day. Ahmad kept her busy.

When Ahmad was three years old, Fatima's second child Lila was born. Lila had beautiful blue eyes and blond curly hair. Fatima's sadness over the loss of her family receded as she was loved by her children and husband.

One day during the time of the Taliban, Jan Muhammad left the house for his work. That was the last day of his life. The Taliban killed him.

Fatima cried with her in-laws at the loss of her husband and their son. But her in-laws were so upset they told Fatima this was her fault. She was bad luck. She had married their son because they had lost another son. They told Fatima that she was in their house because of baad. So they told Fatima they never wanted to see her face again. She was to leave with her children and never return.

Fatima was a 19-year-old woman with a five-year-old son and a year-old daughter. She had no place to go. She went to her uncle's house and asked him for help. Her uncle took her in, but

Fatima soon found out that he had plans for her.

Fatima's uncle found a man who would buy Fatima but not her children, because he did not want his family to know that Fatima had previously been married. When Fatima's uncle told her that she was to be married and her children were not part of the deal, Fatima fell into a deep depression. She begged and pleaded with her uncle. She did not want to be married again. She could not live without her children. But her uncle had taken the money and did not want to give it back.

Twice, Fatima tried to kill herself, but did not succeed either time.

As Fatima's desolation deepened, her uncle's family held many discussions and decided that they would adopt Ahmad. This was a monetary decision. In two years, Ahmad would be seven years old and would be able to work on the street and make money for them.

But no one wanted Lila. She was girl and considered useless, too young to work and too young to sell for marriage.

Finally Lila was sold to someone from a European country as an adoption. As Fatima was separated from her children, she cried and screamed. No one listened to her voice.

# My School for Street Kids
by *Massoma*

Herat province has many poor families who send their young
children out to work every day instead of to school. You can find
girls making carpets at age five or six and young boys working the
streets washing windshields and selling socks or chewing gum.
They earn fifty Afghanis per day, which is enough to buy bread.
I had been working as a journalist for five years when one day I
was touring the streets interviewing these children for a story.
Most were afraid to talk to me, but the few who did said they
didn't go to school because they couldn't afford school supplies.
Not long after this, I began thinking that we needed to have a
school for poor children and orphans.

My heart told me we should find a way to educate the children
for as many as twelve years, but I knew the cost would be very
high. I calculated the necessary budget to put 100 students in
school at more than U.S. $1,000 per month, but my entire salary
of $820 was not going to cover that. I talked about it with my
family, and my father promised to help me.I wrote a letter to the
Education Department and asked for permission to establish a free
private school for poor and orphaned children. It took about one
year to get the school registered with the Ministry of Education, and
I had to go twice to Kabul.

But finally we were registered. We rented a house to use for $100
per month and we identified twenty children, ages five and six,
who wanted to attend the school. At first, families didn't want
to register the children because they had no money for school
clothes and books, so I spent all of my salary and bought

materials and uniforms for all the children. We had five plastic chairs and one desk, and we purchased a rug for the students to sit on. We found qualified teachers. All of our applicants required a salary, so we budgeted $100 per teacher per month. Finally we put up our sign on the door saying Payam-e Danesh, which means Message of Knowledge. We opened our school in March 2010. When the school opened, some of the students didn't know how to behave, and for others, attendance was erratic. But after a while, the teachers did well with inspiring the students to come and learn.

Now, about a year and a half later, Payam-e Danesh has moved to a better location in a market. We have seventy students and five teachers, the headmaster, literacy and embroidery teachers, and a cleaner. We also now offer some literacy and child-raising instruction to the mothers of our students.

When I see the students' development, it makes me very happy to have been able to help create this school and lead the children toward a better future. The students' lives have improved. They were street children and now they are normal school students. We still face many challenges. We have orphan students who often come to school with empty stomachs. We can provide only dry bread for them. All of the students attend for free. If we have money in our pockets we will give children twenty Afghanis because sometimes their parents complain about their children in school and not working. I cannot afford all of this, but Afghan children need an education to help build their country and I will try to keep them in school until they graduate in twelve years.

## Seasons
*by Elay*

I still remember the winters of my childhood. We spent every winter vacation in Jalalabad, one of the warmest provinces of east Afghanistan. In early mornings, the sky was blue, the sun shining and oranges glowed among green leaves. A smooth wind would blow over the narcissus flowers, spreading the scent of the flowers and of orange trees all over our house. Once the scent washed over me, I couldn't stay in bed any longer. Then I would notice the sound of someone making nan (bread) in the tandoor (a special oven for baking nan). The smell of fresh nan took me to Paradise. I will never forget those sunny mornings of Jalalabad's winter.

I loved spring too, as a child, and the cloudy skies of Kabul, the heavy rain of April, the perfume of the blossoms and grass. spring was the season of beginnings and of change. It meant the start of the school year, new classes, new classmates and probably new friends. I always enjoyed the long, fresh rainy days of spring. When I was a kid, spring in Afghanistan meant everything was green and fresh, roads were paved, and weather was not dusty. I would look from my bedroom window to the white and light pink blossoms in the big yard of the Kabul Polytechnic Institute which stood in front of our house. I could see the trees wave in the breeze, and smell the perfumes of the rose flowers. I always counted days and nights until I could see spring, especially the first day of the school.

Since I grew up in a very happy and joyful family, I never used to hate anything or anyone. Then, on a beautiful summer day in

1979, my father, two brothers and two uncles were captured by the Communist government of Afghanistan and jailed, simply because my father was a famous Afghan. I will never forget that dark day of my life. It changed our family's future. Since then, one part of my heart still waits to welcome spring, but another part is reluctant and averse to accepting spring's arrival.
I still love early mornings of Jalalabad's winter. I like spring, but I can't say anymore that I love that season.

## If I Don't Write
*by Roya*


I asked my soul last night,
What happens to you if you don't write?
My soul was in deep thought
I said again,
Answer me...
Pardon me!
I asked if you don't write,
What will happen?


My soul's eyes were full of tears.
She sat in front of me and said,
I can't imagine what will happen
But I can understand when I don't write
I am like a dry river.
Fishes say goodbye.
I am like a thirsty tree waiting for water in a desert —
I am like an orphan child searching love of parents —
I am like a broken lover —
I am like a blasted Kabul street full of blood.


When I can't write,
It is hard to say —
But it is my only identity.
I can't stop writing because
When I can't talk —
When I am very alone,
I am not alone.

With my writings I write about
Things I can't talk about.
When I write
I feel fresh
I wear my favorite dress of my desires,
Sit under the tree of my thoughts
And I write and write.
I stop?
Maybe
When I am not able to breathe.
When...

## My Twilight Wish
*by Hasiba*

Waiting for the sunrise
Reminded me of my innocent wish
In the pleasant silence of the night
I took a ride with my wish
To the top of a fresh green hill
Surrounded by the twilight and silence of the night
I found myself lying down on the grass and facing the sky
The rising moon was at its fullest
The addition of the beauty was with the sparkling stars
The cold air breeze
Embraced my skin so deeply
I felt it in my heart
And sensation poured out of my eyes
Was the twilight what I waited for so long?
No sound heard
No existence felt, but yes
The twilight everywhere
Yes I could feel my wish so close
Yes I could feel the night
Yes I could spend hours on this thought
But the soft spoken sunrise brought me back
From my innocent wish
With a golden morning greeting.

## What the AWWP means to the women writers:

I took my pen to write and at first I was afraid: what to write? about what? But this was a project to write about everything, and I took the pen; I didn't write from outside of my heart, I began to write about whatever was in my heart... The writing project gave me a voice, the project gave me courage to appear as a woman, to tell about my life, to share my pains and experiences. I wonder how big the change in my destiny is because of your work and this project. Who would trust an online class, a writing project, to change a destiny and a faith? AWWP gave me the power to feel I am not only a woman; it gave me a title, an Afghan woman "writer." ... I took the pen and I wrote and everything changed. I learned if I stand, everyone will stand, other women in my country will stand. —Roya

I am writing from Farah, a province in western Afghanistan with a low level of education, and still many men do not like that I write and don't know why I write. They have tried to stop me from writing, but I never gave up. I will do it more and more and show what I've tolerated as a woman and how much Afghan people suffer in their lives. I have thousands of words in my heart to tell the world in thanks to the Afghan Women's Writing Project. —Seeta

AWWP is my heart book where I can share my every moment of life and my people's problems without any fear, where I can say the truth. AWWP is not only valuable for me. It is the voice of all Afghan women who can't write here. We write on behalf of them, to share their stories, and to try to show them their value and rights, and by this way to bring peace to our country, which is the dream of all Afghans. —Shogofa

What does AWWP mean to me? That Afghan women can share their opinions freely on the project, that now no one can prohibit them from sharing their ideas with the world. In the past, Afghan women didn't even have the right to speak with a strange man. This project supports Afghan women by showing they are as important as other women in the world. It shows the world that even though Afghan women faced lots of problems, they didn't lose their ability or courage. It shows the kindness of American women who spend their precious time working for the development of their Afghan sisters. —Sabira

It is freedom of speech into action! We can speak out about our way of life, our desires and the things we regret or like in our culture, without fear of getting in trouble. It gives people the real picture of what it takes to be an Afghan. It helps the outside world understand Afghan society far better than just hearing the news. It is the voice of Afghanistan. We women in the program are lucky. —B. Fatima A.

Made in the USA
Charleston, SC
14 March 2014